The Story
of the
LINCOLN
MEMORIAL

By Natalie Miller

Illustrations by Tom Dunnington

CHILDRENS PRESS, CHICAGO

Library of Congress Catalog Card Number: AC 66-10304

Copyright ©, 1966, Childrens Press, Inc.
All rights reserved. Printed in the U.S.A.
Published simultaneously in Canada

15 16 17 18 19 20 21 22 23 24 25 R 75

Plans were made to build a huge memorial to Abraham Lincoln in the city of Washington. People were to send money to pay for it.

This was just two years after Lincoln had been shot. The news of the memorial traveled slowly. It went by sailing ships and river boats. Little wood-burning trains carried it as far as they went. Stagecoaches took it to outposts in the West. It clicked over the new telegraph line to California.

Money began to come to Washington. Many people sent as much as twenty-five cents. This was a lot of money in 1867, a hundred years ago. Sometimes a man worked all day for that much.

"We'll build a three-sided monument seventy feet high," said the committee. "There will be six generals on horseback at the base. On the second level there will be twenty-one statesmen and important people. On top of the whole thing there will be a giant-size statue of Lincoln signing the Emancipation Proclamation."

This news traveled slowly, too.

"That's not what we want," said the people.

Congress promised that all the damaged and captured cannons would be melted down for the statues when the fund reached $100,000.

"Statues of whom?" asked the people. "Which statesmen? Which generals?" Everyone had a favorite. There were many arguments, and the money stopped coming in. The goal of $100,000 was never reached, and the whole idea quietly faded away.

Many people who had sent hard-earned money never saw a memorial to Lincoln. More than fifty years went by before one was built.

During these years Congress was busy with other things. The railroad was inching its way across the

country and helping to open up the West. Business was booming. The city of Washington was growing. Buildings were springing up wherever there was room for them.

The American Institute of Architects became alarmed. They went to see President Theodore Roosevelt. They said, "Our beautiful city is being ruined. We must have a plan to follow or Washington will be a hodge-podge of buildings."

"You are right," said the President. He set up a Park Commission to find a good plan.

The men studied other capital cities of the world. They studied American cities. They found and dusted off the plans that Pierre L'Enfant had made for Washington city a hundred years earlier. These were just what they wanted.

L'Enfant had planned a spacious mall, an open stretch of grass and trees, from Capitol Hill to the Potomac River. There was to be a memorial of some kind at the water's edge.

"That would be the place for the Lincoln Memorial," said the committee in the report to Congress in 1902.

"What, down in that swampland?" said Congressman Joe Cannon. "With all those mosquitoes, it would catch a fever and shake itself down."

Again the plans for a memorial were pushed aside. However, the land by the river was being drained and filled to become a park someday.

A few years later the powerful automobile makers had a bill introduced in Congress. They wanted a highway built from Washington to Gettysburg. They would call it the Lincoln Memorial Highway.

Railroad men were quick to present a bill suggesting that a square in front of the Union Station would make a better memorial.

The architects joined in the argument. They begged that the spot by the river be used.

At last, in 1911, Congress chose the site on the Potomac and asked a fine architect, Henry Bacon, to design the building.

Once Mr. Bacon had the job to do, it became his whole life. He thought of nothing else for the ten years it took to complete the memorial. No task was too big or too small if it would make this building more perfect.

"It shall be a shining Greek temple of pure white marble, housing only a statue of Lincoln. It must be the most perfect statue of the man that human hands can design. It must almost seem to have a soul," he explained to the committee.

FOUR SCORE AND SEVEN YEARS
AGO OUR FATHERS BROUGHT FORTH
ON THIS CONTINENT A NEW NATION
CONCEIVED IN LIBERTY AND DEDICA-
TED TO THE PROPOSITION THAT ALL
MEN ARE CREATED EQUAL ·
NOW WE ARE ENGAGED IN A GREAT
CIVIL WAR TESTING WHETHER THAT
NATION OR ANY NATION SO CON-
CEIVED AND SO DEDICATED CAN LONG
ENDURE · WE ARE MET ON A GREAT
BATTLEFIELD OF THAT WAR · WE HAVE
COME TO DEDICATE A PORTION OF
THAT FIELD AS A FINAL RESTING
PLACE FOR THOSE WHO HERE GAVE
THEIR LIVES THAT THAT NATION
MIGHT LIVE · IT IS ALTOGETHER FIT-
TING AND PROPER THAT WE SHOULD
DO THIS · BUT IN A LARGER SENSE
WE CAN NOT DEDICATE – WE CAN NOT
CONSECRATE – WE CAN NOT HALLOW –
THIS GROUND · THE BRAVE MEN LIV-
ING AND DEAD WHO STRUGGLED HERE

Lincoln's Gettysburg Address would be carved on one side wall of the chamber. His Second Inaugural Address would be carved on the other. These would be separated from the statue area by columns.

The committee liked Mr. Bacon's ideas, and on February 12, 1914, ground was broken for the building.

One year later, on Lincoln's birthday, huge cranes swung the seventeen-ton cornerstone into place. This hollow stone had two copper boxes sealed into it. They contained a Bible, a story of Lincoln's life, his autograph, copies of state papers, and other interesting things. In the simple ceremony, an American flag was unfurled over the stone as it was lowered into position.

Slowly Mr. Bacon's temple began to take shape. Colorado marble, famous for its whiteness, came by rail across the country. Mr. Bacon watched as the great marble drums were placed one on top of another to form the thirty-six columns around the building. He saw the names of the thirty-six states that had been in the Union during Lincoln's time carved above the columns.

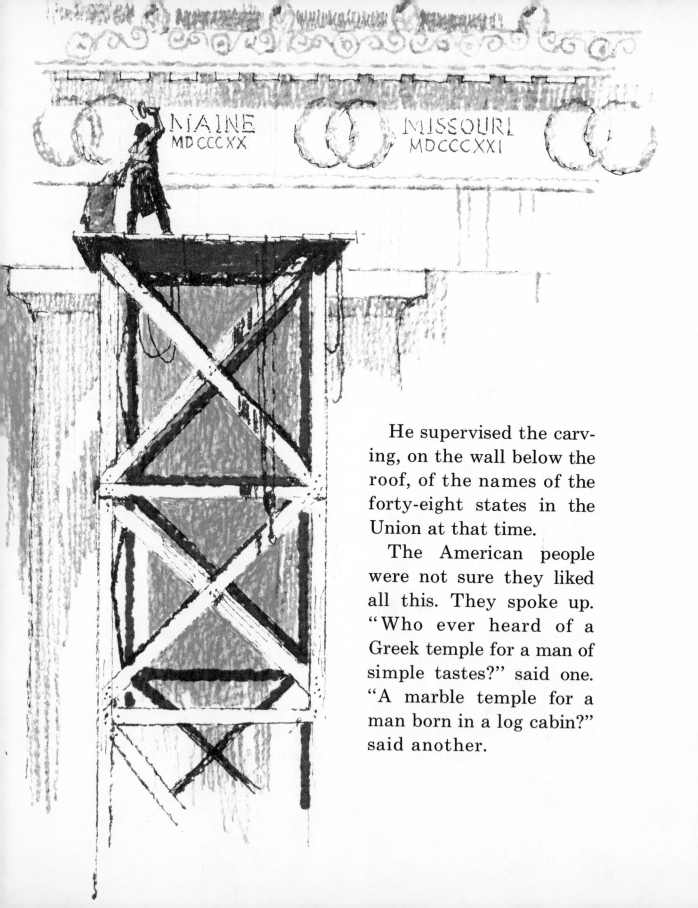

MAINE
MDCCCXX

MISSOURI
MDCCCXXI

He supervised the carving, on the wall below the roof, of the names of the forty-eight states in the Union at that time.

The American people were not sure they liked all this. They spoke up. "Who ever heard of a Greek temple for a man of simple tastes?" said one. "A marble temple for a man born in a log cabin?" said another.

Henry Bacon paid no attention. Other artists came to his defense. "What other kind of building would you want?" they asked. "Egyptian? Roman? French? Lincoln belonged to the ages. What is more fitting than the simple classic lines that have survived for more than a thousand years?"

At last it was time to think about the statue of Lincoln. A sculptor must be chosen. Mr. Bacon recommended his lifelong friend, Daniel Chester French.

The two old friends met in Washington to talk about the project. They decided on a seated bronze statue of Lincoln about ten-feet high.

Daniel French went back to his studio in Stockbridge, Massachusetts. He read everything he could find about Lincoln. He wanted to know the man before he began his work.

Mr. French was a mild-mannered, rather frail man of 65. He was a famous sculptor with a long list of beautiful statues to his credit, including one of Lincoln. But this new assignment was the biggest of his life. It must be exactly right.

He had copies of the life mask of Lincoln's face and casts of his hands. He wanted to show Lincoln as President, the Preserver of the Union, for that was his greatest role.

He made many sketches. Then he began to model in clay. He worked on the hands for weeks. He could not get them to look as he wanted them to look.

Then one day he placed his own hand on the arm of a chair, just as he planned to place Lincoln's. He had his studio man cast his hand in plaster as he sat there. It was a long tiresome job, but worth the trouble. It helped him model Lincoln's hands to suit him. Later he received many letters complimenting him on the power and detail of the hands in his Lincoln statue.

In 1918, almost three years after he was commissioned to do the statue, Daniel French completed an eight-foot model. He shipped it to Washington to see how it would look in the great chamber.

Henry Bacon stood there with him as the workmen uncrated it. Even before it was out of the box,
Mr. French was shaking his head sadly. Both men
knew it was much too small. The statue was dwarfed
by the giant columns of the temple.

They took photographs of the model and had two enlargements made. One was eighteen feet high and one was twenty feet. These were mounted on beaverboard and returned to the chamber.

The architect and the sculptor viewed them from all angles as workmen pushed them around and lifted them to pedestals of different heights.

The two friends agreed that the finished statue should be nineteen feet high and that it should rest on a pedestal about ten feet high. They also decided that the statue must be of marble instead of bronze.

"That will make it about the largest marble statue in the world," said Daniel French.

Henry Bacon nodded. "I will add re-inforcements to the floor. The statue will weigh between 150 and 175 tons. And I will make the ceiling of thin marble slabs. That should give a soft glow to your marble statue."

18

Most sculptors have marble cutters do the final piece of statuary for them. A good marble cutter, with special instruments, can copy exactly a piece of sculpture, making it either larger or smaller than the original model.

When Daniel French had a clay model that was exactly what he wanted, he took it to the Piccirilli brothers in New York City. The six brothers and their father had become successful marble cutters since they came from Italy. Their studios covered almost a whole block. Each man was a fine artist and craftsman.

Mr. French knew that these men could copy perfectly the emotions he had managed to portray in his model. But he went to their studios often and climbed around the scaffolding to do a bit of chiseling himself.

When the cutting was almost finished, Daniel French went to Europe for a short time. The brothers promised to have the statue in place in Washington by the time he returned.

There were twenty-eight separate blocks of marble for the statue. When they were placed on top of each other in the Memorial they fit so perfectly it was hard to see the seams.

Meanwhile Jules Guerin had been commissioned to paint the murals at the sides of the building.

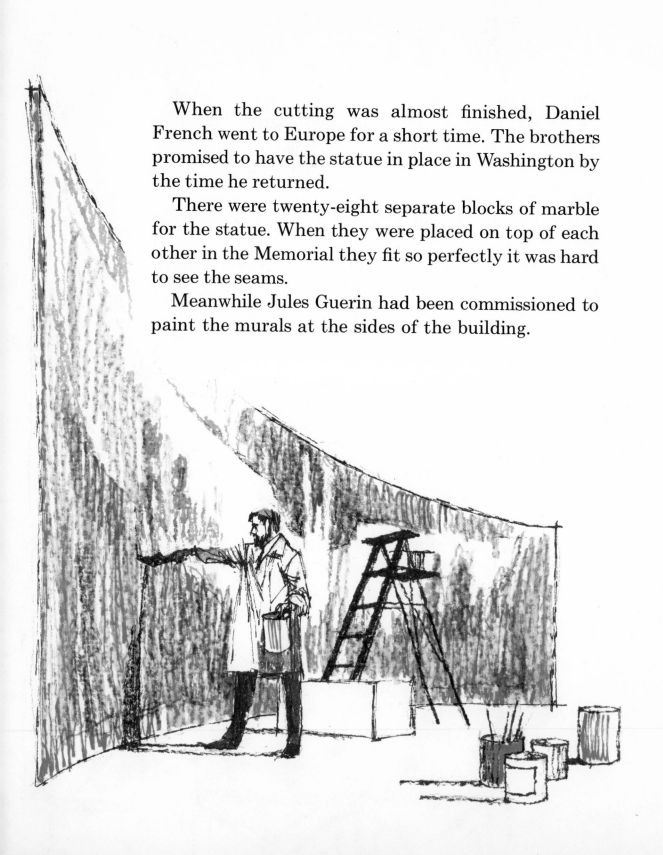

He did not paint them directly on the walls. He painted on huge canvases in his studio. Each weighed about six hundred pounds and he used three hundred pounds of paint. He mixed his paints with white wax and kerosene to make them waterproof. The wax was similar to that found in the tombs of the kings of Egypt that is still pliable today.

No one helped him paint the murals with their forty-six figures for which he used almost as many models. But many workmen had to help him attach the heavy canvases to the walls with white lead and Venetian varnish.

The first mural was finished before the statue arrived. When the picture was in place Henry Bacon and Jules Guerin stood back to see how it looked. The soft glow of light through the ceiling added to its beauty. Henry Bacon smiled with satisfaction. He hoped the light would do as much for the statue.

There are three symbolic pictures on each mural. Over the Gettysburg Address the middle picture shows the Angel of Truth giving freedom to a slave. The picture at the left symbolizes Justice, and the one on the right, Immortality.

On the other wall, one panel shows the Angel of Truth joining the hands of the North and the South. The painting includes figures representing Fraternity and Charity.

While the memorial was being finished, Mr. French was in Europe. He worried about his statue. Were they able to move it into place? Was the size right? How did it look in the memorial?

As soon as he landed in America he hurried to Washington. Breathlessly he climbed the steps of the memorial. He stopped when he saw the head of his Lincoln. The effect was shocking. Instead of the dignity and strength and compassion that he had managed to portray in the model, the marble face looked flat, almost frightened. Slowly he went nearer. The knees loomed large and white, not at all as they were supposed to look.

The scaffolding was still around the statue. A film of dirt, from the sandy ground around the building, covered the white marble.

Immediately Mr. French ordered a bath for his Lincoln.

Day after day the frail sculptor climbed up on the scaffolding. He chiseled a little here with borrowed marble tools, or tinted a little there. He climbed down to study the effect, and went back up again to work. It was no use. The face remained flat and lifeless.

A statue looks best lighted from above. The soft light coming through the thin marble ceiling slabs was no match for the bright sunlight and sky reflected from the pool before the building.

Mr. French had the ceiling slabs coated with paraffin. But this did not help.

During the winter, whenever he thought he had a solution, Daniel French traveled to Washington to try it. Nothing helped.

"Your statue is majestic," friends told him. But he knew it would never be right until the lighting was changed.

The dedication was set for May 30, 1922. The day was clear and warm. Five hundred invitations had been sent to important people. Thousands more came to the ceremony.

The minister from the church that Lincoln had attended offered a short prayer. The flag was presented by the Grand Army of the Republic. Soft-spoken Dr. Robert R. Moton, Principal of Tuskegee Institute, spoke of the gratitude his fellow Negroes felt toward Lincoln, and of the responsibility that comes with freedom. Edwin Markham read his revised poem about the honored President. Chief Justice William Howard Taft, president of the Lincoln Memorial Commission, told of the struggles to get the Memorial started. Fifty-seven years went by after Lincoln's death before the monument was completed. President Harding accepted the Memorial on behalf of the American people.

Afterwards crowds flocked inside to get a better look at the statue. Daniel French leaned against a column to watch the people. They seemed to sense the presence of Lincoln that filled the building which had the majesty and solemnity of a cathedral.

The shimmering white building in its setting of dark boxwood greenery brought nothing but praise.

It was a triumphant day for Henry Bacon and Daniel French. But Mr. French was not yet satisfied. He had spent seven years on the statue and was willing to spend seven more if he could make it right.

He decided to experiment further with the lighting. He went back to his studio and went to work.

The General Electric Company sent experts to experiment with lights on the model. They said that they could counteract the outside glare, but it would be expensive.

Again Daniel French went to Washington to talk to Mr. Bacon. "It would be costly," said Mr. French, "but I would gladly pay part of it myself."

"Nonsense," replied Mr. Bacon. "Congress will grant the money."

Mr. French had been paid $88,000 for the statue, but his expenses had been staggering. He paid the Piccirilli brothers $46,000 to cut the marble. The pedestal had cost $15,000. He spent $1,350 to have the steps and pedestal polished.

Henry Bacon asked Congress for money for lighting. He was told it was too late to get it in the budget — but possibly next year. There was nothing to do but wait.

Spring came and Washington was bright with flowers. Five hundred guests were invited to dinner under a huge awning near the pool in front of the Memorial. It was in honor of Henry Bacon.

After the dinner and a colorful pageant, Mr. Bacon was rowed down the pool in a barge to the steps of the Memorial. President Harding presented him with the Gold Medal of the Institute of Architects, the highest award the institute could give.

Less than a year later Henry Bacon died and the whole architectural world mourned.

Without his friend to help him, Daniel French felt that the statue would never be properly lighted.

However, others took up the fight for him. One of these was "Uncle Joe" Cannon who had objected to building a memorial in that "swampland." And at last, seven years after the dedication ceremony great floodlights, installed back of ceiling slats, shone down on the seated Lincoln.

The effect was stunning. The statue was no longer an immense, cold piece of marble. A compassionate, thoughtful Lincoln looked down on the people.

A small boy tried to climb up in the statue's lap. "He looks so lonesome," the lad explained when the guard took him down. Postmen often bring letters addressed to Mr. Lincoln, Lincoln Memorial.

When "Uncle Joe" Cannon retired after fifty years in Congress, he said, "If I return to Washington it will be to walk down the mall and stand looking up at the greatest American that ever lived."

Shortly after the lights had been installed, Daniel French saw his statue for the last time. It was a soft April night. He stood at the bottom of the marble steps that looked like a waterfall in the moonlight. Before him in the chamber sat the kindly Lincoln he had tried to create, the President, the statesman.

Mr. French walked up to read the words on the wall behind Lincoln's head.

IN THIS TEMPLE
AS IN THE HEARTS OF THE PEOPLE
FOR WHOM HE SAVED THE UNION
THE MEMORY OF ABRAHAM LINCOLN
IS ENSHRINED FOREVER.

Slowly Daniel Chester French walked away. He was content that he had done his best. He felt humble, too, for the privilege of creating the statue for the place of honor in Henry Bacon's shining, beautiful Memorial.

IN THIS TEMPLE
AS IN THE HEARTS OF THE PEOPLE
FOR WHOM HE SAVED THE UNION
THE MEMORY OF ABRAHAM LINCOLN
IS ENSHRINED FOREVER

About the Author: Natalie Miller was born in Maine, grew up in Massachusetts, and majored in history at Beaver College in Pennsylvania. Since 1941 hers has been an Army family, living in many of the 50 states and in Germany and Japan. Mrs. Miller's husband is presently assigned as Professor of Military Science at Cornell University.

About the illustrator: Tom Dunnington grew up in Iowa and Minnesota. He began his art training in Indiana and continued it at the Art Institute and at the American Academy of Art in Chicago. He has five children, lives in Elmhurst, west of Chicago, and works full time as a free-lance illustrator of books. He has had a special, personal interest in this book because Daniel Chester French was his great-uncle.